Deliciously Lean

SALADS FOR
ALL SEASONS

Deliciously Lean

SALADS FOR ALL SEASONS

SAFEWAY/GOOD HOUSEKEEPING

Published exclusively for
Safeway
6 Millington Road, Hayes, Middlesex UB3 4AY
by Ebury Press
A division of Random House
20 Vauxhall Bridge Road
London SW1V 2SA

First published 1993

Edited by Felicity Jackson and Miren Lopategui
Designed by Peartree Design Associates
Photography by James Murphy
Food stylist Janet Smith
Photographic stylist Róisín Nield

The paper in this book is acid-free

Typeset by Textype Typesetters, Cambridge
Printed in Italy

ISBN 0 09 182110 X

─────────── COOKERY NOTES ───────────

All spoon measures are level unless otherwise stated.
Size 2 eggs should be used except when otherwise stated.
Granulated sugar is used unless otherwise stated.

The oven should be preheated to the required
temperature unless otherwise stated.

CONTENTS

FOREWORD

....

SALADS FOR ALL SEASONS is one of a stunning new series of beautifully illustrated cookery books created exclusively for Safeway customers, containing a mouthwatering collection of *Good Housekeeping* salad recipes.

The Good Housekeeping Institute is unique in the field of food and cookery, and every recipe has been created and double-tested in the Institute's world-famous kitchens.

With today's emphasis on healthy eating, salads are perfect for any meal, and this book contains a varied choice of starter, snack or main course salads.

Mayra Fraser

COOKERY EDITOR
GOOD HOUSEKEEPING

INTRODUCTION

The days when a salad consisted of tired lettuce leaves, a sliced tomato and a limp piece of cucumber are over – or at least they should be. Supermarkets now positively abound with brilliant displays of fruits and vegetables.

To start with, cast your eye over the varieties of lettuces now on offer. New, interesting, well-flavoured leaves are appearing all the time, from the ubiquitous Cos and Iceberg, to exotica like the frilly leaved frisée or curly endive, or the russet brown Feuille de Chêne (Oak Leaf). Other interesting varieties worth looking out for are batavia, Lollo Rosso (Red Lollo) and Quattro Stagioni (Four Seasons) and the bitter, dark red radicchio.

Lamb's lettuce, a delicate green leaf which is not a true lettuce, but a weed native to Europe, is now cultivated mainly in France and makes a delicious addition to any salad bowl. Roquette (arugula), with its distinctive, peppery taste, is not a lettuce but a salad herb. It's experiencing a revival and makes a spectacular salad dressed simply with olive oil.

Choosing and storing salad ingredients

Whichever variety you choose, the leaves should be firm and crisp with no signs of browning or insect damage. To prepare, pull off and discard any damaged outer leaves. Transfer the clean leaves to polythene bags and store in the salad drawer in the refrigerator.

Combining different ingredients

Not all salads are based on lettuce. The recipes in this book show you how to combine meat, fish, vegetables, fruits, nuts, seeds, pulses and pasta in a whole range of dishes that include starters, main meal salads, vegetarian salads and simple side salads using both summer and winter ingredients.

SALAD DRESSINGS

A salad is rarely complete without a light coating of dressing, whether it's a tart, fresh-tasting vinaigrette, a smooth, creamy mayonnaise or simply a squeeze of lemon juice.

The foundation of most good dressings is the oil. Olive oil, with its distinctive flavour, has long been regarded as the all-purpose salad oil. Virgin olive oil, which has a dark green colour and a strong rich aroma has the best flavour.

The rich and mellow nut oils - walnut, hazelnut and sesame – are becoming more popular. They are delicious blended with the lighter oils, such as sunflower oil. Walnut oil is considered by many to be the best of all for salad dressings. Nut oils tend to go rancid quickly; once opened, store them in the refrigerator.

Most dressings combine oil with some acidic element. Lemon, mustard and yogurt can all provide the essential tartness, but the ingredient most often chosen is vinegar, which comes in lots of flavours. The proportion of oil to vinegar varies according to taste.

Wine and cider vinegars are suitable for salad dressings. Wine vinegars range from light delicately flavoured ones to rich, mellow red wine vinegars. Sherry vinegar is a dark, full-flavoured variety. Balsamic vinegar is a dark, mellow vinegar with an excellent flavour. Although expensive, only a small amount is needed to lend a superb flavour to a dressing. Vinegars flavoured with garlic, herbs such as tarragon, or fruit such as raspberries, add unusual flavours to dressings.

A salad based on robust ingredients like root vegetables, pulses, rice, pasta, dried fruit, seeds, nuts and grains, can have the dressing added when everything is freshly cooked and still warm. Leave to cool. stirring occasionally, so that the flavours have time to be absorbed and mellow. Delicate leaf- and herb-based salads tend to flop if dressed too soon, so get everything ready and toss together at the last minute.

SALAD STARTERS

....

Summer starters for dinner parties and
lunches should be light and refreshing.
Just enough to set the mouth watering and
the taste buds tingling. A salad fits the bill
perfectly, and in this chapter you can
choose from a selection of fish, meat, fruit,
vegetable and cheese salads to
complement whatever main course you
are serving.

Top: Tomato, Melon and Mint Salad with Herb Vinaigrette (page 16)
Bottom: Smoked Mackerel Salad with Yogurt and Orange (page 22)

MANGO AND PRAWN SALADS

SERVES 4

2 ripe mangoes
225 g packet peeled ready-to-eat prawns
6 × 15 ml tbs very low-fat fromage frais
2 × 15 ml tbs reduced calorie mayonnaise
grated rind of 1 lime
2 × 5 ml tsp lime juice
1 × 5 ml tsp snipped fresh chives
salt and pepper
mixed salad leaves
prawns with their shells on and slices of ripe mango,
to garnish

1 Slice each mango twice lengthways, either side of the stone. Cut the flesh in the segments lengthways and widthways without breaking the skin, then push the skin inside out to expose the cubes of flesh. Slice off and remove the flesh in neat cubes and put in a bowl. Peel the remaining centre sections and cut the flesh away from the stones into cubes. Add to the bowl.
2 Add the peeled prawns, fromage frais, mayonnaise, lime rind and juice, chives, salt and pepper to the mango and mix together.
3 Arrange the mixture on a bed of salad leaves on individual serving plates. Serve garnished with the whole prawns and mango slices.

141 CALORIES PER SERVING

ITALIAN MIXED SALAD

SERVES 6

3 thin slices of Italian salami
3 thin slices of Mortadella sausage
1 head radicchio or a small lettuce,
cleaned and trimmed
3 thin slices of Parma ham, cut in half
2 hard-boiled eggs, quartered
3 tomatoes, sliced
198 g can of mussels in vinegar, drained
(optional)
½ × 290 g jar of artichoke hearts in oil, well drained
(optional)
green and black olives, stoned, and fresh herbs,
to garnish
crusty bread, to serve

1 Ease any skin or rind off the salami and the Mortadella sausage with your fingers. Cut each slice in half.
2 Place a bed of radicchio or lettuce on a large serving platter. Arrange the pieces of salami, Mortadella, Parma ham, hard-boiled eggs, tomatoes and mussels and artichoke hearts, if using, on top. Garnish with the olives and fresh herbs.
3 Cover tightly with clingfilm and refrigerate for at least 2 hours. Leave at cool room temperature for about 20 minutes before serving.

208 CALORIES PER SERVING

VARIATION
Instead of radicchio lettuce, a 280 g jar of sweet and sour peppers can be used.

Top: Mango and Prawn Salads
Bottom: Italian Mixed Salad

CRISP VEGETABLE SALAD

SERVES 6

salt and pepper

450 g (1 lb) broccoli

225 g (8 oz) asparagus

150 g (5 oz) mangetout

450 g (1 lb) fennel

DRESSING

6 × 15 ml tbs olive oil

2 × 15 ml tbs white wine vinegar

1 × 5 ml tsp Dijon mustard

pinch of sugar

1 Put a large saucepan of salted water on to boil. Meanwhile, trim the broccoli into bite-sized florets. Cut off and reserve the asparagus tips. Trim about 2.5 cm (1 in) off the bottom of the stalks. Top and tail the mangetout and cut the fennel into large chunks, reserving the feathery tops for the dressing.

2 When the water is bubbling furiously, plunge the asparagus tips and mangetout in for 1 minute. Meanwhile, fill a basin with cold water and add some ice cubes.

3 Remove the asparagus tips and the mangetout from the pan with a slotted spoon and plunge into the cold water for 1 minute. Lift out of the water and drain well.

4 Add the asparagus stalks, broccoli and fennel to the boiling water and simmer for 3 minutes. Transfer into the cold water and cool for 2-3 minutes, drain well. Toss all the vegetables together in a bowl. Cover and chill.

5 Whisk all the dressing ingredients together with the finely chopped fennel tops. Season.

6 About 30 minutes before serving the salad, gently toss the vegetables and dressing together. Serve at room temperature.

170 CALORIES PER SERVING

CAPONATA

SERVES 6

1 large aubergine

salt and pepper

3 × 15 ml tbs olive oil

1 large onion, skinned and sliced

50 g can anchovies and capers, drained and sliced

2 celery sticks, sliced

400 g can tomatoes

50 g (2 oz) stoned black olives

1 × 5 ml tsp sugar

1 × 15 ml tbs wine vinegar

100 g can tuna steak in brine, drained and flaked

chopped fresh parsley, to garnish

Italian bread, to serve

1 Cut the aubergine into 2.5 cm (1 in) pieces, then put in a colander, sprinkling each layer with salt. Stand the colander on a plate. Cover with a small plate, put a weight on top, and leave for 30 minutes to extract the bitter juices. Rinse under cold running water and pat dry with absorbent kitchen paper.

2 Heat the oil in a large non-stick saucepan, add the aubergine and fry until browned on both sides. Remove from the pan with a slotted spoon.

3 Add the onion to the pan and fry for 5 minutes until softened. Add half of the anchovies and capers, the celery, tomatoes, olives, sugar and vinegar. Season with pepper. Bring to the boil then simmer for 20 minutes, stirring occasionally and breaking up the tomatoes. Stir in the aubergine.

4 Pile into a serving dish. Leave to cool, then chill in the refrigerator.

5 To serve, garnish with the remaining anchovies and capers and the tuna and sprinkle with parsley. Serve with Italian bread.

148 CALORIES PER SERVING

Caponata

TOMATO, MELON AND MINT SALAD WITH HERB VINAIGRETTE

SERVES 6

1 ripe melon
450 g (1 lb) tomatoes, peeled, halved and seeded
handful of fresh mint

DRESSING

1½ × 5 ml tsp mustard powder
½ × 5 ml tsp salt
1 × 5 ml tsp sugar
pepper
1 × 15 ml tbs chopped fresh parsley
1 × 15 ml tbs snipped fresh chives
2 × 15 ml tbs oil, preferably a mixture of olive and sunflower
1 × 15 ml tbs wine vinegar

1 Cut the melon in half and scoop out the seeds. Peel the melon and cut it into neat 2.5 cm (1 in) chunks. Cut each tomato half into wedges.
2 Reserve a few mint leaves for garnish. Strip the rest from their stems and chop. Combine with the tomatoes and melon in a bowl.
3 Put the ingredients for the dressing into a screw-topped jar and shake well. Just before serving, pour the dressing over the salad and toss together. Garnish with reserved mint leaves.

167 CALORIES PER SERVING

COOK'S TIP

This is a most colourful summery salad, full of fresh herbs, the flavours of which are absorbed by the melon and tomato. Don't mix in the dressing until shortly before serving; otherwise it tends to get diluted by melon juice.

SALAD OF BAKED GOAT'S CHEESE AND HAZELNUTS

SERVES 6

25 g (1 oz) hazelnuts
12 thin slices of French bread
12 thin slices of goat's cheese
selection of mixed salad leaves, including oak leaf, frisée and radicchio, cleaned and trimmed
3 × 15 ml tbs low-fat French dressing
freshly ground black pepper

1 Place the hazelnuts on a baking tray and toast in the oven at 180°C/350°F/Gas Mark 4 for 10-12 minutes until thoroughly browned. Tip the nuts on to a clean tea-towel and rub off the loose skins. Roughly chop the nuts, then return to the oven for 2-3 minutes until evenly browned.
2 Increase the oven temperature to 220°C/425°F/Gas Mark 7. Arrange the slices of French bread on a baking tray. Top each with a slice of cheese and bake for 10 minutes until the bread is crisp and the cheese hot but not melted.
3 Meanwhile, arrange the salad leaves on six plates.
4 When the cheese and bread are ready, arrange on top of the salad leaves. Sprinkle each with a little of the dressing and the hazelnuts. Grind a little pepper over the top and serve immediately.

235 CALORIES PER SERVING

Salad of Baked Goat's Cheese and Hazelnuts

SHREDDED
COURGETTE
SALAD

SERVES 6

½ head of curly endive

5 × 15 ml tbs natural yogurt

4 × 15 ml tbs reduced calorie mayonnaise

1 × 15 ml tbs snipped fresh chives

1 × 15 ml tbs chopped fresh parsley

1 × 15 ml tbs chopped fresh basil

salt and pepper

675 g (1½ lb) small courgettes

basil sprigs, to garnish

1 Tear the endive into small pieces and divide between six small plates.

2 In a medium bowl, mix together the yogurt, mayonnaise and herbs. Season with salt and plenty of pepper.

Shredded Courgette Salad

3 Just before serving, coarsely grate the courgettes. Add to the dressing and stir together. Spoon on to the individual serving plates and garnish with sprigs of basil.

62 CALORIES PER SERVING

SALAD NIÇOISE

SERVES 6

450 g (1 lb) small new potatoes, scrubbed

salt and pepper

115 g (4 oz) French beans, topped and tailed

2 eggs, hard-boiled

4 ripe tomatoes, roughly chopped

50 g (2 oz) stoned black olives

200 g can tuna steaks in brine, drained and cut into chunks

15 g (½ oz) canned anchovies, drained

2 × 15 ml tbs extra virgin olive oil

1 × 15 ml tbs white wine vinegar

pinch of sugar

pinch of mustard powder

1 × 5 ml tsp lemon juice

mixed salad leaves

1 Cook the potatoes in boiling salted water for 15-20 minutes, or until tender. Cook the French beans in boiling salted water for 3 minutes, or until just tender.

2 Cut the hard-boiled eggs into wedges. Toss together the potatoes, beans, eggs, tomatoes, olives and tuna and top with the anchovies.

3 Whisk together all the remaining ingredients except the salad leaves to make a dressing. Season to taste. Pile the vegetable mixture on a bed of mixed salad leaves and then pour the dressing over the top.

201 CALORIES PER SERVING

COOK'S TIP

This salad is delicious served hot or cold. If serving cold, cool the vegetables before tossing.

Salad Niçoise

COMPOSED SALAD
WITH
TAPÉNADE

SERVES 6

TAPÉNADE

450 g (1 lb) large black olives, stoned

2 garlic cloves, skinned

50 g can anchovies, drained

50 g (2 oz) drained capers

3 × 15 ml tbs olive oil

pepper

SALAD

*selection of mixed salad leaves, such as
corn salad, oak leaf lettuce, radicchio lettuce,
escarole, cleaned and trimmed*

6 canned artichoke hearts, halved

1 bulb of fennel, thinly sliced

1 head of chicory, separated into leaves

3 hard-boiled eggs, shelled and halved

115 g (4 oz) button mushrooms

225 g (8 oz) baby or cherry tomatoes

225 g (8 oz) carrots, peeled and grated

6 × 15 ml tbs low-fat French dressing

1 small French stick, thinly sliced and toasted

1 Put the olives, garlic, anchovies,capers, olive oil and pepper in a blender or food processor and blend until smooth to make the tapénade. Divide the mixture between six small dishes.

2 Arrange the salad ingredients on six large plates and drizzle a little dressing over. Serve with the tapénade and toasted French bread. The anchovy-flavoured tapénade is spread over the bread.

170 CALORIES PER SERVING

WARM SALAD
OF
MUSHROOMS

SERVES 8

*selection of mixed salad leaves, cleaned
and trimmed*

*175 g (6 oz) young spinach leaves, cleaned
and trimmed weight*

*115 g (4 oz) smoked lean bacon, rinded
and cut into thin strips*

4 × 15 ml tbs olive oil

675 g (1½ lb) mushrooms, wiped and thickly sliced

1 garlic clove, skinned and crushed (optional)

salt and pepper

1½ × 15 ml tbs tarragon vinegar

1 Arrange the salad leaves and the spinach on eight plates.

2 Heat a heavy-based frying pan and fry the bacon until the fat runs. Increase the heat and fry for a couple of minutes until crisp. Add the oil and mushrooms and cook over a high heat for 3-4 minutes until the mushrooms are just tender. Add the garlic, if using, and pepper and cook for a minute longer.

3 Using a slotted spoon, remove the mushrooms from the pan and scatter them over the salad leaves. Quickly add the vinegar to the juices remaining in the pan and boil rapidly for 2 minutes. Season with salt and pepper. Pour the juices over the salads and serve immediately.

120 CALORIES PER SERVING

COOK'S TIP

This salad works well with cultivated oyster or shiitake mushrooms or cup mushrooms.

Top: Warm Salad of Mushrooms
Bottom: Composed Salad with Tapénade

SMOKED MACKEREL SALAD WITH YOGURT AND ORANGE

SERVES 4

1 bunch of watercress cleaned and trimmed

175 g (6 oz) smoked mackerel fillets

2 small oranges

6 × 15 ml tbs low-fat natural yogurt

2 × 5 ml tsp creamed horseradish sauce

salt and pepper

4 slices brown toast, to serve

1 Place the watercress on four individual serving plates. Skin the mackerel fillets and divide between the serving plates.

2 Whisk together the grated rind of one orange, 2 × 15 ml tbs orange juice, the yogurt and horseradish. Season to taste. Peel and segment the second orange.

3 Place a few orange segments around the mackerel. Spoon the dressing over and accompany with toast.

170 CALORIES PER SERVING

LEMONY BEAN SALAD

SERVES 4

115 g (4 oz) dried flageolet beans, soaked overnight in enough cold water to cover

3 × 15 ml tbs olive oil

finely grated rind and juice of 1 lemon

1-2 garlic cloves, skinned and crushed

salt and pepper

50 g (2 oz) black olives, stoned and roughly chopped

2 × 15 ml tbs chopped mixed fresh herbs, e.g. basil, marjoram, lemon balm, chives

4 large firm tomatoes

about ¼ × 5 ml tsp raw cane sugar

lemon wedges, to garnish

1 Drain the beans. Place in a saucepan with plenty of water. Bring to the boil and boil for 10 minutes, then cover and simmer gently for 1¼ hours or until the beans are tender.

2 Drain the beans, transfer to a bowl and immediately add the oil, lemon rind and juice, garlic and salt and pepper to taste. Stir well to mix, then cover and leave for at least 4 hours.

3 Add the olives to the salad with the herbs.

4 To skin the tomatoes, put them in a bowl, pour boiling water over and leave for 2 minutes. Drain, then plunge into a bowl of cold water. Remove them one at a time and peel off the skin.

5 Slice the tomatoes thinly, then arrange on four serving plates. Sprinkle with sugar, salt and pepper to taste. Pile the bean salad on top of each plate. Serve chilled, garnished with lemon wedges.

219 CALORIES PER SERVING

RED PEPPER AND FENNEL SALAD

SERVES 4–6

3 × 15 ml tbs olive oil

1 onion, skinned and finely chopped

1 garlic clove, skinned and crushed

4 red peppers, seeded and sliced into rings

salt and pepper

2 small bulbs of fennel, quartered lengthways and feathery tops reserved for garnish

2 × 15 ml tbs water

1 Heat the oil in a large saucepan. Add the onion and garlic, and cook gently for about 5 minutes. Stir in the peppers and seasoning.

2 Arrange the fennel in the pan. Add the water. Cover and cook gently for 30 minutes until the fennel is tender. Cool before serving, garnished with finely chopped feathery fennel tops.

164-109 CALORIES PER SERVING

Top: Red Pepper and Fennel Salad
Bottom: Lemony Bean Salad

FISH AND
SHELLFISH SALADS

....

*What could be more delicious than
a lightly cooked, melt-in-the-mouth, fish
salad. The ones in this chapter make
a delicious meal for lunch or supper.
It's important to cool any hot fish quickly,
then cover and chill it in the refrigerator.
Remove from the refrigerator about
30 minutes before serving for
maximum flavour.*

Smoked Trout and Lentil Salad (page 26)

MARINATED KIPPER SALAD

SERVES 4

450 g (1 lb) kipper fillets, skinned

1 small onion, skinned

1 bay leaf

pepper

4 × 15 ml tbs olive oil

grated rind and juice of 1 lemon

1 Cut the kippers lengthways into thin slices. Arrange them in a shallow serving dish.
2 Thinly slice the onion into rings and scatter it over the kippers. Add the bay leaf and pepper.
3 Put the oil, lemon rind and juice in a bowl and whisk well together. Pour the dressing over the kippers, then stir to ensure it is evenly distributed. Cover and leave to marinate in the refrigerator for 24 hours, stirring occasionally. Serve chilled.

304 CALORIES PER SERVING

SMOKED TROUT AND LENTIL SALAD

SERVES 8

DRESSING

115 ml (4 fl oz) olive oil

6 × 15 ml tbs white wine vinegar

1 × 5 ml tsp ground coriander

½ × 5 ml tsp caster sugar

2 × 5 ml tsp Dijon mustard

salt and pepper

SALAD

335 g (12 oz) green lentils

2 onions, skinned and sliced into wafer-thin rings

675 g (1½ lb) smoked trout fillets

roquette or other salad leaves, to garnish

1 Whisk together all the dressing ingredients and set aside.
2 Pick over the lentils and rinse well. Place in a saucepan, cover with cold water, bring to the boil, cover and boil rapidly for 10 minutes. Lower the heat and simmer for 5-10 minutes until the lentils are tender but still *al dente* (firm to the bite). Drain well, place in a non-metallic bowl and stir in the dressing and onion rings. Cover and leave in a cool place overnight.
3 To serve, roughly flake the smoked trout. Spoon the lentils on to eight individual serving plates. Top with pieces of smoked trout. Garnish with roquette or other salad leaves.

365 CALORIES PER SERVING

MEDITERRANEAN SEAFOOD SALAD

SERVES 4

1 red pepper, seeded

3 × 225 g packets fresh seafood cocktail

3 × 15 ml tbs olive oil

1 × 15 ml tbs lemon juice

1 garlic clove, skinned and crushed

2 × 15 ml tbs chopped celery leaves

1 × 15 ml tbs flat leaf parsley plus sprigs, to garnish

salt and pepper

selection of mixed salad leaves

prawns with their shells on, to garnish

hot garlic bread, to serve

1 Grill, peel and chop the red pepper.
2 Put the seafood in a shallow serving dish.
3 Put the oil, lemon juice, garlic, celery leaves, parsley, salt and pepper in a large bowl. Whisk the dressing until well blended, then pour over the fish and toss together. Leave in the refrigerator for 2-3 hours before serving.
4 Arrange the salad leaves on four individual serving plates. Add the chilled fish and garnish with the prawns and parsley sprigs. Serve with hot garlic bread.

300 CALORIES PER SERVING

Mediterranean Seafood Salad

HOT, SWEET AND SOUR FISH AND FLAGEOLET SALAD

SERVES 4

335 g (12 oz) trout fillets

1 large orange

150 ml (5 fl oz) water

2 × 15 ml tbs red wine vinegar

2 × 15 ml tbs soy sauce

2 × 15 ml tbs tomato purée

1 × 15 ml tbs clear honey

1 × 5 ml tsp hot chilli powder

2.5 cm (1 in) piece fresh root ginger, peeled and grated

1 garlic clove, skinned and crushed

salt and pepper

400 g can flageolet beans, drained and rinsed

½ iceberg lettuce

handful of coriander leaves

1 Put the fish fillets in a large shallow pan, and add the juice of half the orange and the water. Bring the water to a simmer, cover and cook the fish gently for 6-8 minutes, until just cooked.

2 Using a fish slice, lift the fish out of the pan. When cool enough to handle, remove the skin, then flake the fish into large chunks.

3 To make the dressing, mix the remaining orange juice with the vinegar, soy sauce, tomato purée, honey, chilli powder, ginger and garlic. Season with salt and pepper.

4 Mix the beans and fish with the dressing while still warm. Leave to cool.

5 Shred the lettuce into bite-sized pieces and mix with the beans and fish. Serve sprinkled with coriander leaves.

244 CALORIES PER SERVING

VARIATION

Omit the flageolet beans, if preferred, and serve the fish and dressing on lettuce leaves.

PIQUANT PURPLE SALAD

SERVES 4

450 g (1 lb) baby new potatoes, scrubbed

4 × 15 ml tbs olive oil

2 × 15 ml tbs white wine vinegar

salt and pepper

450 g (1 lb) whiting fillets, skinned

2 × 15 ml tbs milk

150 ml (5 fl oz) water

2 large pickled dill cucumbers or 4 pickled gherkins

½ cucumber

175 g (6 oz) cooked beetroot

selection of red salad leaves
(radicchio lettuce, lollo rosso, oak leaf lettuce)

2 × 15 ml tbs capers

6 anchovy fillets

2 × 15 ml tbs chopped fresh dill

1 Cook the potatoes in boiling salted water for 15-20 minutes, until tender. Drain.

2 Whisk the oil and vinegar together and season with salt and pepper. Pour it over the warm potatoes and leave to cool.

3 Cut the fish into small strips about 1 cm (½ in) wide. Put the milk in a pan with the water. Bring to the boil, then add the fish and cook gently for about 3-4 minutes, until just cooked. Drain carefully and leave to cool.

4 Slice the pickled dill cucumbers and the fresh cucumber and mix with the potatoes. Peel the beetroot and cut into chunks.

5 Arrange the salad leaves on a serving dish. Spoon on the potato mixture, then the fish and the beetroot. Mix lightly together. Sprinkle with the capers, anchovies and dill.

395 CALORIES PER SERVING

Top: Hot, Sweet and Sour Fish and Flageolet Salad
Bottom: Piquant Purple Salad

NEW POTATO AND PRAWN SALAD

SERVES 4

450 g (1 lb) new potatoes, scrubbed

50 ml (2 fl oz) olive oil

2 × 15 ml tbs red wine vinegar

salt and pepper

1 red pepper

225 g (8 oz) ripe red tomatoes

335 g (12 oz) large, peeled, cooked prawns

flat leaf parsley sprigs, to garnish

1 Cook the potatoes in boiling salted water for 15-20 minutes until tender, then drain. While still warm, halve or quarter the potatoes, depending on size.

2 Whisk together the oil, vinegar and seasoning in a large bowl. Stir in the warm potatoes and leave to marinate for 20-30 minutes, stirring occasionally.

3 Meanwhile, dice the pepper, discarding the seeds; halve, seed and roughly chop the tomatoes. Stir these into the cold potatoes with the prawns. Season to taste. Cover and chill for at least 2 hours.

4 Leave at room temperature for at least 30 minutes before serving and stir well to mix. Garnish with parsley sprigs.

312 CALORIES PER SERVING

FRESH SARDINES WITH ORANGE AND HERB DRESSING

SERVES 4

12 sardines

1 orange

3 × 15 ml tbs olive oil

1 × 15 ml tbs dry white wine

pepper

baby spinach leaves, washed

½ × 15 ml tbs chopped fresh mint

orange slices, to garnish

1 Wash the sardines well, remove scales and gut if preferred. Dry on absorbent kitchen paper and arrange in a non-metallic dish.

2 Using a zester, pare the rind of the orange into shreds and set aside. Squeeze out the juice of the orange into a bowl. Add the oil, wine and pepper. Whisk together until well blended, then pour the dressing over the sardines. Cover and leave to marinate in a cool place for at least 2 hours.

3 Line a grill pan with foil, then grill the sardines for 3-4 minutes on each side, basting with some of the dressing. Return the cooked sardines to the dish containing the dressing. Leave to cool, then chill in the refrigerator.

4 To serve, arrange the sardines on a bed of baby spinach leaves on four plates and spoon over the dressing. Sprinkle over the mint and reserved orange shreds, then garnish with orange slices.

389 CALORIES PER SERVING

Top: Fresh Sardines with Orange and Herb Dressing
Bottom: New Potato and Prawn Salad

MEAT SALADS

....

*Summer main courses can be a problem if
you are not well prepared. This chapter
brings you a whole selection of meat
salads, including warm salads and spiced
salads, that can either be partly prepared
in advance or are very quick and easy to
prepare, to help you stay out of the kitchen
in the good weather.*

*Top: Marinated Beef and Olive Salad (page 42)
Bottom: Duckling Salad with Ginger Dressing (page 40)*

GOLDEN CHICKEN WITH SPICED WHEAT

SERVES 6

1 × 15 ml tbs mango chutney

1 × 15 ml tbs mild curry paste

2 × 5 ml tsp ground turmeric

50 ml (2 fl oz) olive oil

4 skinless chicken breast fillets,
total weight about 565g (1¼ lb)

2 × 15 ml tbs white wine vinegar

175 g (6 oz) cracked wheat

salt and pepper

2 × 15 ml tbs snipped fresh chives

175 g (6 oz) cherry tomatoes,
mixed yellow and red, if possible

1 bunch of salad onions, roughly chopped

marjoram leaves, to garnish (optional)

1 Mix together the chutney, curry paste and turmeric. Stir in 50 ml (2 fl oz) oil. Cut the chicken into bite-size pieces and toss into the mixture. Cover and marinate for 30 minutes, or overnight in the refrigerator.

2 Spread the chicken pieces over a foil-lined grill pan. Cook under a hot grill in batches for 10-12 minutes until the chicken is cooked through and golden brown. Transfer to a bowl with the pan juices and stir in the remaining oil and the vinegar. Leave to cool.

3 Meanwhile, place the cracked wheat in a bowl and pour over enough boiling water to cover. Leave to soak for 30 minutes to 1 hour until all of the water has been absorbed and the grains are soft. Stir once or twice and drain well. Season. Stir in the chives.

4 Drain the oil mixture from the chicken and stir into the wheat. Spoon on to a platter.

5 Halve the tomatoes. Mix together with the salad onions and chicken and spoon over the cracked wheat. Garnish with marjoram leaves, if wished.

337 CALORIES PER SERVING

COOK'S TIP

To prepare ahead, follow the recipe to the end of step 3, then keep everything covered in the refrigerator overnight. The next day, drain the oil mixture from the chicken and stir into the wheat. Finish off with the tomatoes and salad onions.

CHICKEN STIR-FRY SALAD

SERVES 4

450 g (1 lb) chicken breast fillets, skinned
and cut into very thin strips

2 × 5 ml tsp sesame oil

2 garlic cloves, skinned and crushed

2 cm (¾ in) piece of fresh root ginger,
peeled and grated

1 red chilli, seeded and chopped

3 × 15 ml tbs light soy sauce

½ head of Chinese leaves, cleaned, trimmed
and torn into bite-sized pieces

½ head curly endive, cleaned, trimmed
and torn into bite-sized pieces

1 × 15 ml tbs sunflower oil

pepper, to taste

radish roses, to garnish (optional)

1 Put the chicken strips in a bowl. Add the sesame oil, garlic, ginger, chilli and soy sauce. Stir well and leave to marinate for 15 minutes.

2 Meanwhile, arrange the Chinese leaves and endive on a serving platter or individual plates.

3 Heat the sunflower oil in a large frying pan or wok and cook the chicken mixture over a high heat for 3-4 minutes, stirring constantly, until the chicken is cooked through.

4 Spoon the mixture over the leaves. Season and serve immediately, garnished with radish roses, if liked.

215 CALORIES PER SERVING

Top: Golden Chicken with Spiced Wheat
Bottom: Chicken Stir-Fry Salad

CHICKEN LIVER SALAD

SERVES 2

selection of mixed salad leaves
1 × 15 ml tbs olive oil
225 g (8 oz) frozen chicken livers,
thawed and trimmed
1 × 15 ml tbs snipped fresh sage
2 × 15 ml tbs balsamic vinegar
salt and pepper

1 Arrange the salad leaves on two plates.
2 Heat the oil in a non-stick frying pan, add the chicken livers and sage and cook for 2-3 minutes, stirring all the time. Using a slotted spoon, remove from the pan and place on top of the salad leaves.
3 Add the vinegar to the pan and season with salt and pepper. Heat, stirring well to deglaze the pan, then pour over the salads. Serve at once.

248 CALORIES PER SERVING

COOK'S TIP
Frozen chicken livers make a useful stand-by ingredient to keep in the freezer for making all sorts of hot and cold dishes. Make sure they have completely thawed before you cook them.

WARM CHICKEN AND LIVER SALAD

SERVES 4

565 g (1¼ lb) boneless chicken breast fillets
2 × 15 ml tbs clear honey
2 × 15 ml tbs wholegrain mustard
3 × 15 ml tbs lemon juice
2 × 15 ml tbs olive oil
salt and pepper
115 g (4 oz) chicken livers, trimmed
selection of mixed salad leaves and
crusty brown bread, to serve

1 Skin the chicken fillets and cut the flesh into bite-sized pieces. Place in a bowl with the honey, mustard, lemon juice, oil and seasoning. Stir well to mix. Cover and leave to marinate in the refrigerator overnight.
2 Cut the livers into small pieces. Place the chicken in a foil-lined grill pan with half the marinade. Grill for about 5 minutes. Add the livers and remaining marinade and baste well. Continue grilling for a further 5 minutes or until the meat is cooked.
3 Divide the chicken mixture between individual serving plates lined with salad leaves. Accompany with crusty brown bread.

307 CALORIES PER SERVING

VARIATION
For a change, try adding some chopped cucumber or red-skinned onion to the salad.

COOK'S TIP
The mustard seeds are left whole in wholegrain mustard, giving a lovely crunchy texture to the dressing for this salad.

Top: Chicken Liver Salad
Bottom: Warm Chicken and Liver Salad

HONEYED CHICKEN AND THYME SALAD

SERVES 8

8 skinless chicken breast fillets, total weight about 1.4 kg (3 lb)

225 ml (8 fl oz) olive oil

4 × 5 ml tsp Dijon mustard

2 × 15 ml tbs white wine vinegar

2 × 5 ml tsp caster sugar

2 × 15 ml tbs clear honey

grated rind and juice of 1 lemon

3 × 15 ml tbs chopped fresh thyme

salt and pepper

1 ripe pear, weighing about 175 g (6 oz)

Savoy cabbage or salad leaves, to serve

1 Place the chicken under a hot grill for 10-12 minutes until cooked through and golden brown. Allow to cool, then slice.

2 Whisk together the next eight ingredients. Slice the pear and add to the dressing.

3 Place the chicken in a shallow dish and pour the dressing over it.

4 Cover and refrigerate for at least 1 hour but preferably overnight. (Spoon the dressing over the chicken occasionally.) Serve the marinated chicken on a bed of Savoy cabbage or salad leaves.

239 CALORIES PER SERVING

VARIATION

Lightly cooked sliced courgettes and mangetout can be added with the pear.

Honeyed Chicken and Thyme Salad

SALAMAGUNDY

SERVES 8

1 roasted duckling

1 roasted chicken

450 g (1 lb) carrots, cut into strips

salt and pepper

450 g (1 lb) potatoes, peeled

450 g (1 lb) peas, cooked

1 cucumber, sliced

115 ml (4 fl oz) low-fat French dressing

225 g (8 oz) tomatoes, thinly sliced

4 celery sticks, thinly sliced

flat leaf parsley sprigs, to garnish

1 Remove and discard the skin from the duckling and chicken, then carefully remove the flesh and cut into thin strips, about 5 cm (2 in) long.

2 Cook the carrots in boiling salted water for 10-15 minutes until just tender; drain. Cook the potatoes in boiling salted water for 15-20 minutes until tender. Drain and leave to cool, then dice.

3 Place the potatoes and peas in the bottom of a large oval platter to give a flat base. Arrange a layer of cucumber on top, following the oval shape of the platter.

4 Pour over a little dressing. Next, arrange a layer of carrot, slightly inside the first layer. Top with more layers of chicken meat, tomato slices, celery and duck meat. Sprinkle each one with dressing. Continue layering until all the ingredients are used. Garnish with parsley sprigs.

235 CALORIES PER SERVING

Salamagundy

DUCKLING SALAD WITH GINGER DRESSING

SERVES 6

6 boneless duckling breasts, each
weighing 115 g (4 oz)
salt and pepper
selection of mixed salad leaves
toasted sesame seeds, trimmed chives
and orange slices,
to garnish

GINGER DRESSING

3 salad onions, trimmed
50 ml (2 fl oz) olive oil
2 × 15 ml tbs lemon juice
grated rind and juice of 1 orange
1 × 5 ml tsp caster sugar
5 cm (2 in) piece of fresh root ginger,
peeled and grated
1 garlic clove, skinned and crushed
1 × 5 ml tsp sesame oil
2 × 5 ml tsp soy sauce

1 Prick the duckling breasts all over with a sharp knife; sprinkle with salt. Place skin side down on a wire rack over a roasting tin. Cook at 200°C /400°F/Gas Mark 6 for 10 minutes. Turn and cook for 20 minutes until the duckling is tender and the skin is crisp. Cool, then slice thickly.
2 Tear the salad leaves into small pieces and arrange on a platter.
3 Finely chop the salad onions, then combine all the dressing ingredients.
4 Toss the duckling with half of the dressing and arrange on the salad. Garnish with the sesame seeds, chives and orange slices. Serve with the remaining dressing.

320 CALORIES PER SERVING

WARM DUCK SALAD

SERVES 8

8 boned duckling breasts, each weighing
about 115 g (4 oz)
2 × 15 ml tbs ground coriander
2 × 5 ml tsp ground ginger
2 × 5 ml tsp ground mace
1 garlic clove, skinned and crushed
75 ml (3 fl oz) fresh orange juice
75 ml (3 fl oz) olive oil
salt and pepper
½ × 15 ml tbs clear honey
1 × 15 ml tbs red wine vinegar
½ × 15 ml tbs Dijon mustard
selection of mixed salad leaves
to line the dish
about 20 stoned black olives

1 Remove the skin from the duck. Mix together the coriander, ginger, mace and garlic with 2 × 15 ml tbs each of orange juice and oil. Season.
2 Spread spice mixture on both sides of duck breasts and place in a shallow ovenproof dish. Roast at 200°C/400°F/Gas Mark 6 for 15-20 minutes until duckling is tender and top browned.
3 Meanwhile, whisk together honey, vinegar, mustard and remaining orange juice and oil. Season to taste. Wash salad leaves, dry and arrange on a shallow platter.
4 Lift the duck breasts out of the pan juices, slice neatly and arrange on the salad leaves. Scatter over olives and spoon over the dressing.

327 CALORIES PER SERVING

COOK'S TIP

If wished, the duck can be cooked in advance and served cold. If only large duck breasts are available, cut them in half to give two fillets.

Warm Duck Salad

BEEF SALAD WITH HORSERADISH DRESSING

SERVES 2

2 × 5 ml tsp creamed horseradish sauce

2 × 15 ml tbs low-fat French dressing

salt and pepper

selection of mixed salad leaves, cleaned and trimmed

3 tomatoes, sliced

175 g (6 oz) cold roast beef

mint leaves, to garnish

1 Stir the horseradish sauce into the French dressing. Season well and mix thoroughly.

2 Arrange the salad leaves and sliced tomatoes on two serving plates.

3 Trim the beef, slices and place on top of the salad. Spoon the dressing over the salad and garnish with mint leaves.

205 CALORIES PER SERVING

WARM LAMB SALAD

SERVES 4

4 × 115 g (4 oz) leg of lamb steaks

2 × 5 ml tsp vegetable oil

115 ml (4 fl oz) low-fat French dressing

4 × 15 ml tbs fresh orange juice

1 × 15 ml tbs wholegrain mustard

salt and pepper

335 g (12 oz) leeks, thinly sliced

335 g (12 oz) spring greens, trimmed and thinly sliced

75 g (3 oz) bean sprouts

25 g (1 oz) walnut pieces, toasted

1 Brush the lamb steaks with oil and grill for about 4 minutes on each side. Cut into thick slices.

2 Whisk together the French dressing, orange juice, mustard and seasoning. Heat in a large saucepan, then add the leeks and spring greens.

Cook over high heat for 3-4 minutes until the vegetables are just tender, stirring frequently.

3 Add the bean sprouts, toasted walnuts and lamb and continue to cook for 1 minute. Serve warm.

352 CALORIES PER SERVING

MARINATED BEEF AND OLIVE SALAD

SERVES 4

450 g (1 lb) rolled lean brisket

1 bay leaf

6 peppercorns

450 g (1 lb) French beans, trimmed and sliced into halves

salt and pepper

1 large bunch of salad onions, trimmed and sliced diagonally into thick pieces

12 black olives, stoned and quartered

3 × 15 ml tbs soy sauce

4 × 5 ml tsp lemon juice

1 Put the beef, bay leaf and peppercorns in a saucepan. Add enough water to cover. Bring to the boil, cover and simmer gently for about 1 hour until the meat is tender. Leave to cool in the cooking liquid for about 2 hours.

2 Cook the beans in boiling salted water for 5-10 minutes until just tender. Drain well, rinse under cold water and drain again thoroughly.

3 Drain the beef and trim off the fat. Slice thinly and cut into 4 cm (1½ in) long shreds.

4 Put the beef in a bowl and add the salad onions, olives, beans, soy sauce and lemon juice. Toss well together, then season with pepper to taste. Cover and chill in the refrigerator for about 30 minutes before serving.

226 CALORIES PER SERVING

Top: Beef Salad with Horseradish Dressing
Bottom: Warm Lamb Salad

PORK AND MUSHROOM SALAD

SERVES 8

2 pork fillets or tenderloins, well trimmed and
each weighing about 335 g (12 oz)

2 × 15 ml tbs sunflower oil

225 g (8 oz) small button mushrooms, wiped

50 ml (2 fl oz) water

juice of ½ lemon

1 small onion, skinned and finely sliced

1 small green pepper, seeded and
finely shredded

10 green olives, stoned

115 ml (4 fl oz) low-fat natural yogurt

¼ × 5 ml tsp mustard powder

salt and pepper

salad leaves, to serve

fresh marjoram or mint leaves, to garnish

1 Cut the pork into 1 cm (½ in) slices on the diagonal, then cut each slice into neat strips, about 5 cm × 0.6 cm (2 in × ¼ in).

2 Heat the oil in a large frying pan, add half the pork and fry quickly to seal the meat. Repeat with the remaining meat, then return all to the pan. Lower the heat and slowly cook for about 10-15 minutes until very tender. Using a slotted spoon, lift the meat out of the pan and leave to cool.

3 Add the mushrooms to the pan with the water and lemon juice. Cook, stirring, for 1-2 minutes until just tender. Using a slotted spoon, remove the mushrooms from the pan and leave to cool.

4 Put the onion and green pepper in a pan of cold water, bring to the boil and simmer for 1-2 minutes until just tender. Drain and cool under running cold water. Stir into the pork with the cooled mushrooms and olives.

5 Mix the yogurt with the mustard, season to taste and stir into the pork mixture. Cover and chill for at least 3 hours.

6 Stir the salad well before serving on a bed of salad leaves, garnished with the marjoram or mint leaves.

330 CALORIES PER SERVING

SMOKED VENISON AND ORANGE SALAD

SERVES 2

3 small blood oranges

1 × 15 ml tbs olive oil

1 × 5 ml tsp lemon juice

2.5 cm (1 in) piece of fresh root ginger,
peeled and finely grated

salt and pepper

115 g (4 oz) smoked Scottish wild venison

sprigs of flat leaf parsley, to garnish

1 Grate the rind from 1 orange into a small bowl. Add the oil, lemon juice, 3 × 15 ml tbs orange juice, ginger and salt and pepper.

2 Using a serrated knife, remove all the peel and pith from 2 oranges then, holding the oranges over the bowl, divide into segments, discarding the pips and as much of the membrane as possible. Reserve the juice.

3 Arrange the slices of venison, in loose folds, with the orange segments on two plates. Garnish with parsley sprigs.

4 Just before serving, whisk the orange dressing with the reserved orange juice until well blended, then serve separately in a small jug.

242 CALORIES PER SERVING

Top: Smoked Venison and Orange Salad
Bottom: Pork and Mushroom Salad

POTATO, SALAMI AND OLIVE SALAD

SERVES 4

900 g (2 lb) small potatoes, scrubbed

salt and pepper

low-fat French dressing to taste

115 g (4 oz) salami, roughly chopped

115 g (4 oz) cooked ham, roughly chopped

12 black olives, stoned and halved

6 × 15 ml tbs Greek-style natural yogurt

1 × 5 ml tsp wholegrain mustard

chopped fresh parsley, to garnish (optional)

1 Boil the potatoes in slightly salted water for 20 minutes until tender. Drain, then cool slightly before cutting into chunks and moistening with French dressing.

2 Add the salami, ham and olives. Stir the yogurt and mustard in, and season to taste. Sprinkle with chopped fresh parsley, if liked.

372 CALORIES PER SERVING

ITALIAN PEPPERONI SALAD

SERVES 4–6

50 ml (2 fl oz) olive oil

1 onion, skinned and chopped

1 red pepper, seeded and sliced

1 garlic clove, skinned and chopped

225 g (8 oz) arborio (Italian risotto) rice

pinch of saffron threads

600 ml (20 fl oz) hot chicken stock

1 × 15 ml tbs balsamic vinegar

pepper

150 g (5 oz) pepperoni sausage, skinned (if wished) and thinly sliced

25 g (1 oz) stoned black olives

flat leaf parsley sprigs, to garnish

1 Heat 1 × 5 ml tsp oil in a large non-stick saucepan. Add the onion, pepper and garlic and fry for 5 minutes until soft.

2 Stir the rice in and cook for 1 minute. Stir in the saffron threads and hot stock. Bring to the boil, then simmer for about 15 minutes, stirring occasionally, until the rice is just tender and has absorbed all the stock. Place in a large shallow serving dish and leave until cold.

3 In a bowl, put the remaining oil, the vinegar and pepper.

4 Just before serving, add the sausage to the cold rice. Whisk the dressing until well blended then pour over the rice and toss gently together. Stir in the olives, then garnish with the parsley.

369-246 CALORIES PER SERVING

COOK'S TIP

Arborio rice is an Italian short grain rice which readily absorbs liquid without becoming too soft. It is this property which gives a risotto its distinctive creamy texture. It is equally good when used in a salad.

Top: Potato, Salami and Olive Salad
Bottom: Italian Pepperoni Salad

VEGETARIAN SALADS

....

Salads don't necessarily have to be based on lettuce leaves. In this chapter you will find a selection of vegetarian salads that also include all kinds of vegetables, pulses, grains and rice, as well as dairy foods and tofu (bean curd). Some make perfect accompaniments for vegetarian main courses, others make a meal in themselves.

Top: Herb Omelette Salad (page 50)
Bottom: Vegetable Salamagundy (page 55)

HERB OMELETTE SALAD

SERVES 4

4 eggs, beaten

2 × 15 ml tbs fines herbs

(parsley, tarragon, chives and chervil)

or other chopped fresh herbs

2 × 15 ml tbs water

salt and pepper

butter or margarine

1 large red pepper, seeded and
cut into strips

1 large green pepper, seeded and
cut into strips

1 small bulb of fennel, trimmed and
thinly sliced

1 bunch of salad onions, trimmed and
cut into strips

½ cucumber, cut into thin strips

low-fat French dressing to taste

1 Beat the eggs with the herbs and water. Season with salt and pepper. Heat a knob of butter or margarine in an omelette pan and use the eggs to make two thin, lightly set omelettes. Turn out on to a sheet of greaseproof paper, roll up and leave to cool slightly. Toss the remaining ingredients together.

2 Thinly slice the omelette and toss over the prepared salad ingredients. Serve immediately.

157 CALORIES PER SERVING

WARM WHEAT AND FETA SALAD

SERVES 6

175 g (6 oz) cracked wheat

300 ml (10 fl oz) boiling water

115 g (4 oz) feta cheese

2 salad onions

4 tomatoes

3 × 15 ml tbs low-fat French dressing

3 × 15 ml tbs olive oil

grated rind and juice of 1 lemon

salt and pepper

4 × 15 ml tbs chopped fresh mixed herbs
such as mint, parsley and oregano

a few vine leaves to garnish

25 g (1 oz) stoned black olives,
to garnish

lime wedges, to garnish

1 Put the cracked wheat in a bowl and pour over the boiling water. Leave to soak for 30 minutes.
2 Meanwhile, cut the cheese into small cubes. Trim and finely slice the onions. Finely chop the tomatoes.
3 Put the French dressing, oil, lemon rind and juice, salt if required and pepper in a bowl and mix well together. Stir in the chopped herbs.
4 Add the cheese, onions and tomatoes to the soaked cracked wheat. Pour the dressing over the wheat and toss well together.
5 Line a serving dish with the vine leaves then pile the salad on top. Garnish with the olives and lime wedges and serve warm.

245 CALORIES PER SERVING

COOK'S TIP
Canned vine leaves are available in a 450 g can.

Warm Wheat and Feta Salad

HOT SPICED
CHICK-PEA SALAD

SERVES 4

1 × 15 ml sunflower oil
1 onion, skinned and roughly chopped
2 × 5 ml tsp ground turmeric
1 × 15 ml tbs cumin seeds
450 g (1 lb) tomatoes, roughly chopped
2 × 430 g cans chick-peas, drained
1 × 15 ml tbs lemon juice
4 × 15 ml tbs chopped fresh coriander
salt and pepper
coriander leaves, to garnish

1 Heat the oil in a saucepan and sauté the onion for about 10 minutes or until golden brown.
2 Add the turmeric and cumin seeds and cook, stirring, for 1-2 minutes before adding the remaining ingredients, except the coriander leaves.
3 Continue cooking for about 2 minutes, stirring frequently until heated through. Adjust the seasoning and serve garnished with fresh coriander leaves.

311 CALORIES PER SERVING

PASTA SALAD
WITH
BASIL AND CHEESE

SERVES 4

175 g (6 oz) tricoloured pasta spirals
75 g (3 oz) mangetout, trimmed
6 cauliflower florets, very finely sliced
3 salad onions, trimmed and sliced
small handful of fresh basil leaves
1 × 15 ml tbs chopped fresh parsley
75 g (3 oz) fresh Parmesan cheese,
cut into small cubes
5 × 15 ml tbs low-fat French dressing
fresh basil leaves, to garnish

1 Cook the pasta in boiling salted water for 8-10 minutes, or according to packet instructions. Drain and cool under cold running water.
2 Steam the mangetout for 3 minutes, then cool under cold running water. Slice them very finely diagonally.
3 Mix the vegetables with the pasta, and fold in the herbs and cheese. Stir in the dressing.
4 Cover the salad tightly and leave to stand in a cool place (not the refrigerator) for a minimum of 5 hours and a maximum of 24 hours, stirring it from time to time so that all the flavours mingle thoroughly. Serve garnished with basil leaves.

268 CALORIES PER SERVING

VARIATION
If you like a strongly flavoured dressing, add a clove of crushed garlic to the French dressing.

COOK'S TIP
This vegetable and pasta salad is perfect for meals in the garden, as well as for picnics – just take some fresh basil leaves wrapped in clingfilm with you to decorate the salad before serving.

Top: Pasta Salad with Basil and Cheese
Bottom: Hot Spiced Chick-Pea Salad

CHICORY AND CELERY SALAD

SERVES 4

1 eating apple, cored and chopped
1 head of celery, trimmed and sliced
1 cooked beetroot, peeled and sliced
2 heads of chicory, sliced
1 punnet of mustard and cress, trimmed
½ × 5 ml tsp prepared English mustard
½ × 5 ml tsp sugar
4 × 15 ml tbs low-fat natural yogurt
2 × 5 ml tsp white wine vinegar
salt and pepper
3 hard-boiled eggs, shelled

1 Lightly mix the apple, celery, beetroot and chicory together with the mustard and cress in a large salad bowl.
2 To make the dressing, whisk the mustard, sugar, yogurt and vinegar together. Season to taste. Pour over the salad and toss together so that everything is coated in the dressing.
3 Cut the eggs into halves or slices and add to the salad. Serve at once.

114 CALORIES PER SERVING

Left: Wheat, Celery and Pepper Salad
Right: Chicory and Celery Salad

VEGETABLE SALAMAGUNDY

SERVES 8

50 g (2 oz) green lentils

225 g (8 oz) French beans, trimmed

225 g (8 oz) mangetout, trimmed

salt and pepper

225 g (8 oz) beef tomatoes, sliced (optional)

225 g (8 oz) cherry tomatoes, halved

1 yellow pepper, seeded and cut into strips

½ small head of celery, trimmed and sliced

1 small onion, skinned and thinly sliced

2 eating apples, sliced

black olives

115 ml (4 fl oz) low-fat French dressing

fresh herbs, to garnish

1 Boil the lentils vigorously for 10 minutes, then cover, lower the heat and cook for a further 15-20 minutes until just tender. Drain and leave to cool. Blanch the beans and mangetout in boiling salted water for 2 minutes. Drain, rinse under cold running water and drain.

2 Arrange all the ingredients, except the dressing and garnish, on one or two large platters in a symmetrical pattern. Sprinkle with the dressing and garnish with the fresh herbs.

---

75 CALORIES PER SERVING

COOK'S TIP

Salamagundy is an old English supper dish which dates back to the eighteenth century. Traditionally it contains a varied mixture of meats. This version makes the most of fresh colourful vegetables. Any other vegetables in season can be added. Add hard-boiled eggs or nuts, if liked.

WHEAT, CELERY AND PEPPER SALAD

SERVES 4

115 g (4 oz) cracked wheat

300 ml (10 fl oz) boiling water

175 g (6 oz) green pepper, halved, seeded and roughly chopped

115 g (4 oz) celery, trimmed and thickly sliced

3 × 15 ml tbs olive oil

2 × 15 ml tbs lemon juice

1 × 5 ml tsp Dijon or wholegrain mustard

pinch of caster sugar

salt and pepper

½ × 5 ml tsp ground turmeric

pinch of cumin seeds

50 g (2 oz) salted peanuts

sprigs of fresh herbs, to garnish

1 Place the cracked wheat in a bowl and pour over the boiling water. Leave to soak for 10-15 minutes.

2 Place the pepper and celery in a bowl. Whisk together all the remaining ingredients except the peanuts and stir into the pepper and celery. Add the cracked wheat and peanuts. Stir well; adjust seasoning before serving, garnished with fresh herbs.

---

292 CALORIES PER SERVING

VARIATION

Substitute 75 g (3 oz) brown rice, cooked and cooled, for the cracked wheat.

ORIENTAL TOFU AND BEAN SALAD

SERVES 4

2 × 15 ml tbs dark soy sauce

2 × 15 ml tbs dry sherry

2 × 15 ml tbs orange juice

2.5 cm (1 in) piece of fresh root ginger,
peeled and finely grated

black pepper

175 g (6 oz) smoked firm tofu

1 × 15 ml tbs sesame or vegetable oil

1 garlic clove, skinned and finely chopped

115 g (4 oz) mangetout, trimmed

4 salad onions, finely sliced

½ head of Chinese leaves

430 g can black-eye beans, drained and rinsed

1 In a bowl, put the soy sauce, sherry, orange juice, ginger and pepper and mix together. Cut the tofu into 1 cm (½ in) cubes and stir it into the mixture. Leave to marinate for 1 hour. Drain the tofu, reserving the marinade.

2 Heat the oil in a large non-stick frying pan. Add the tofu and cook, stirring, for 2 minutes. Add the garlic, mangetout and salad onions and stir-fry for a further 2 minutes. Transfer to a bowl and leave to cool.

3 Finely shred the Chinese leaves. Wash and dry and put in a large salad bowl.

4 Add the beans and reserved marinade to the cold tofu mixture, mix together and pile on top of the Chinese leaves. Carefully toss the salad before serving.

214 CALORIES PER SERVING

SPINACH AND AVOCADO IN YOGURT DRESSING

SERVES 4

225 g (8 oz) spinach, cleaned and
trimmed weight, finely shredded

50 g (2 oz) radicchio lettuce, cleaned,
trimmed and finely shredded

400 g can flageolet beans, drained

1 ripe avocado

4 × 15 ml tbs low-fat natural yogurt

grated lemon rind

1 × 5 ml tsp lemon juice

snipped fresh chives, to garnish

salt and pepper

1 Put the spinach in a bowl, together with the radicchio lettuce and beans.

2 Peel and slice the avocado, removing the stone, and add to the vegetables.

3 To make the dressing, mix the yogurt with the lemon rind and juice, then add the chives and seasoning.

4 Just before serving, stir the dressing through the spinach and avocado until well mixed.

196 CALORIES PER SERVING

Oriental Tofu and Bean Salad

Spinach and Avocado in Yogurt Dressing

SUMMER SALADS

....

Use all the fresh seasonal produce readily available and cheap in the summer months to make these delicious sunny salads. They are all perfect for livening up simple chicken or fish dishes, a plain omelette or a grilled chop. Most of the salads in this chapter could also make a refreshing summer lunch or supper, if served with wholemeal bread spread sparingly with low-fat spread.

Top: Strawberry and Cucumber Salad (page 66)
Middle: Carrot and Pineapple Salad (page 60)
Bottom: Pan-Fried Courgette Salad (page 60)

CARROT AND PINEAPPLE SALAD

SERVES 4

450 g (1 lb) carrots, scrubbed

50 g (2 oz) Edam cheese, coarsely grated

a few raisins or sultanas

a few snipped fresh chives

2 fresh or canned pineapple slices, cut into chunks

low-fat French dressing to moisten

salt and pepper

a little curry paste (optional)

1 Grate the carrots, and place in a bowl.

2 Stir in the cheese, raisins or sultanas, chives and pineapple chunks. Moisten with a little well seasoned French dressing and a little curry paste, if wished.

115 CALORIES PER SERVING

COOK'S TIP

If using canned pineapple in natural juice, and home-made French dressing, use the juice instead of vinegar in the dressing.

PAN-FRIED COURGETTE SALAD

SERVES 4

40 g (1½ oz) blanched almonds

675 g (1½ lb) courgettes

2 × 15 ml tbs olive oil

2 × 15 ml tbs lemon juice

50 g (2 oz) raisins

salt and pepper

sprigs of flat leaf parsley, to garnish

1 Soak the almonds in boiling water for about 10 minutes. Drain and slice. Thickly slice the courgettes diagonally.

2 Heat the oil in a large wok or frying pan. Add the courgettes (in two batches if necessary) and

the almonds. Stir-fry over a high heat for 7-8 minutes, adding a little more oil if necessary, until the courgettes are golden brown and just beginning to soften, but still crunchy.

3 Stir in the lemon juice, raisins and seasoning. Spoon into a bowl and serve cold, but not chilled, garnished with the parsley.

193 CALORIES PER SERVING

SWEET PEPPER AND AUBERGINE SALAD

SERVES 4

2 × 15 ml tbs low-fat French dressing

1 × 15 ml tbs extra virgin olive oil

2 small, fat aubergines, cut into slices

2 large, long red peppers

2 × 5 ml tsp lemon juice

2 × 15 ml tbs chopped fresh basil

1 garlic clove, skinned and thinly sliced

salt and pepper

fresh basil leaves, to garnish

1 Mix together the French dressing and olive oil. Brush the aubergine slices with the dressing mixture and then grill with the whole peppers until blackened all over, turning the aubergine slices and brushing with more dressing. Put in a bowl and immediately cover with a damp tea-towel. Leave until cool enough to handle.

2 Remove the charred skins from the peppers and cut lengthways into quarters, removing the core and seeds and reserving any juices in a bowl. Stir the remaining cooking juices from the grill pan into the bowl, then add the lemon juice, basil, garlic, salt and pepper. Drizzle the mixture over the vegetables. Serve at room temperature, garnished with basil leaves.

122 CALORIES PER SERVING

Sweet Pepper and Aubergine Salad

CHERRY TOMATO SALAD

SERVES 6

2 × 15 ml tbs olive oil

1 × 5 ml tsp balsamic or red wine vinegar

2 × 5 ml tsp wholegrain mustard

salt and pepper

900 g (2 lb) cherry tomatoes, halved

shavings of Parmesan cheese, to serve

fresh basil leaves, to garnish

1 Whisk together the olive oil, vinegar and wholegrain mustard. Season.

2 Toss the tomatoes in the dressing; cover and refrigerate.

3 Just before serving, toss the tomatoes with shavings of Parmesan cheese. Serve garnished with fresh basil leaves.

117 CALORIES PER SERVING

TOMATO AND ARTICHOKE SALAD

SERVES 4

450 g (1 lb) ripe tomatoes

400 g can artichoke hearts

50 g (2 oz) onion or shallots, skinned

1 large clove garlic, skinned and crushed

2 × 15 ml tbs lemon juice

4 × 15 ml tbs olive oil

salt and freshly ground pepper

whole pickled green chillies, to garnish

1 Slice the tomatoes. Drain the artichoke hearts and halve or quarter. Arrange the sliced tomatoes and artichoke hearts on a serving dish.

Top: Tomato and Artichoke Salad
Middle: Cherry Tomato Salad
Bottom: Fennel, Pear and Parmesan Salad

2 Thinly slice the onion. Whisk together the crushed garlic, lemon juice, oil and seasoning. Stir in the onion.

3 Spoon the dressing over the vegetables and garnish with the pickled chillies. Cover and chill for about 30 minutes.

143 CALORIES PER SERVING

FENNEL, PEAR AND PARMESAN SALAD

SERVES 6

2 bulbs of fennel, washed

2 ripe pears, washed and cored

coarsely ground black pepper

50 ml (2 fl oz) olive oil

50 g (2 oz) piece fresh Parmesan cheese,
or mature Cheddar cheese

1 Remove the feathery tops from the fennel and roughly chop them. Set aside. Cut the fennel into wafer-thin slices and arrange on a serving platter.

2 Thinly slice the pears and scatter the slices over the fennel. Season with lots of pepper. Drizzle over the olive oil.

3 Using a swivel potato peeler, pare the Parmesan cheese over the top. Scatter over the chopped fennel tops and serve immediately.

141 CALORIES PER SERVING

MINTED GREENS

SERVES 6

3 × 15 ml tbs chopped fresh mint

50 ml (2 fl oz) olive oil

2 × 15 ml tbs white wine vinegar

grated rind of 1 lemon

1 × 5 ml tsp Dijon mustard

1 × 5 ml tsp caster sugar

225 g (8 oz) podded fresh peas

175 g (6 oz) podded broad beans

salt and pepper

225 g (8 oz) courgettes, thickly sliced

175 g (6 oz) runner beans, trimmed
and halved

1 bunch of salad onions, finely chopped

fresh mint leaves, to garnish

1 Whisk together the mint, olive oil, vinegar, lemon rind, mustard and sugar, then set aside.

2 Place the peas and beans in a saucepan of boiling, salted water. Return to the boil, cook for 3 minutes, add the courgettes and runner beans and boil for a further 1 minute, or until just tender. Drain well, then refresh under cold water so that they retain their colour.

3 Toss the vegetables with the salad onions in the prepared mint dressing, adjust the seasoning and serve immediately, garnished with mint.

147 CALORIES PER SERVING

COOK'S TIP

Any green vegetables can be used in this salad. It's light and fresh and makes a good accompaniment to barbecued meats or poached salmon. It is delicious served just warm but is equally good cold. Don't toss the dressing in until the last minute or you'll find that the vegetables will lose their bright colour.

Minted Greens

CRISP LEAFY SALAD WITH BACON AND WALNUTS

SERVES 4

selection of mixed salad leaves

sprigs of flat leaf parsley (optional)

3 × 15 ml tbs walnut oil

1 × 15 ml tbs balsamic vinegar

1 garlic clove, skinned and crushed

salt and pepper

115 g (4 oz) lean, rindless bacon rashers, diced

50 g (2 oz) walnut pieces

1 Tear any large salad leaves into small pieces and put with the parsley, if using, in a salad bowl.
2 In a small bowl, put the oil, vinegar, garlic, salt and pepper.

3 Fry the diced bacon in its own fat until golden brown, then sprinkle over the salad. Add the walnut pieces.
4 Whisk the dressing together until well blended, then pour over the salad. Toss together and serve at once.

234 CALORIES PER SERVING

COOK'S TIP

A packet of mixed salad leaves containing colourful leaves, such as dark red radicchio, oak leaf and frilly frisée or curly endive, is perfect for this salad. Alternatively, use a few leaves from any whole lettuces of your choice.

Crispy Leaf Salad with Bacon and Walnuts

ICEBERG LETTUCE WITH CREAMY LIME DRESSING

SERVES 4-6

½ an iceberg lettuce

½ cucumber, finely diced

4 × 15 ml tbs reduced calorie mayonnaise

2 × 15 ml tbs very low-fat fromage frais

grated rind and juice of 1 lime

salt and pepper

1 Using a sharp knife, shred the lettuce. Wash and dry and put in a salad bowl. Add the diced cucumber.

2 In a bowl, put the mayonnaise, fromage frais, lime rind and juice and salt and pepper. Mix well together.

3 Spoon the dressing over the salad and toss lightly together just before serving.

54-36 CALORIES PER SERVING

MIXED LEAF AND ALMOND SALAD

SERVES 4

1 small head of radicchio lettuce,
cleaned and trimmed

½ head of oak leaf lettuce,
cleaned and trimmed

½ head of curly endive, cleaned and trimmed

25-50 g (1-2 oz) alfalfa sprouts

3 × 15 ml tbs grapeseed oil

2 × 15 ml tbs white wine vinegar

4 × 5 ml tsp clear honey

salt and pepper

25 g (1 oz) flaked almonds, toasted

1 Wash the salad leaves and shred roughly. Rinse the alfalfa sprouts in a sieve or colander. Pat the salad leaves and the alfalfa sprouts dry with absorbent kitchen paper.

2 To make the dressing, whisk together the grapeseed oil, white wine vinegar and honey. Season.

3 Toss the salad leaves, alfalfa sprouts, almonds and dressing together in a large salad bowl. Serve immediately.

165 CALORIES PER SERVING

COOK'S TIP

For the crispest salad, toss the leaves and dressing together at the very last minute.

STRAWBERRY AND CUCUMBER SALAD

SERVES 4

1 small cucumber

freshly ground black pepper

200 ml (7 fl oz) unsweetened apple juice

225 g (8 oz) strawberries, hulled

fresh mint sprigs, to garnish

1 With the prongs of a fork, scrape down the sides of the cucumber to make a ridged effect. Slice the cucumber very thinly and lay in a shallow dish. Sprinkle with the freshly ground pepper to taste. Pour 150 ml (5 fl oz) of the apple juice over and chill in the refrigerator for 15 minutes.

2 Slice the strawberries if large; otherwise, cut them in half. Put into a small bowl and pour the remaining apple juice over them. Chill in the refrigerator for 15 minutes.

3 Drain the cucumber and strawberries and arrange them attractively on a serving dish. Garnish with mint sprigs.

38 CALORIES PER SERVING

Top: Iceberg Lettuce with Creamy Lime Dressing
Bottom: Mixed Leaf and Almond Salad

CUCUMBER AND WATERCRESS SALAD

SERVES 6

2 × 15 ml tbs white wine vinegar

1 × 5 ml tsp sugar

1 × 15 ml tbs olive oil

4 × 5 ml tsp lemon juice

salt and pepper

1 cucumber, weighing about 335 g (12 oz)
and cut into matchstick-sized pieces

1 small bunch of salad onions, trimmed
and sliced

1 bunch of watercress

25 g (1 oz) chopped walnuts

1 Whisk together the vinegar, sugar, olive oil and lemon juice. Season with salt and pepper. Toss the cucumber and salad onions together in the dressing. Cover and refrigerate until required.

2 Divide the watercress into sprigs. Rinse and drain, then refrigerate in a polythene bag.

3 Just before serving, toss the cucumber and the salad onions again. Sprinkle the walnuts over and surround with watercress sprigs.

72 CALORIES PER SERVING

SPICED POTATO SALAD

SERVES 6

900 g (2 lb) small new potatoes, scrubbed

salt and pepper

150 ml (5 fl oz) Greek-style natural yogurt

¼ × 5 ml tsp ground coriander

¼ × 5 ml tsp ground cumin

2 green chillies, seeded and chopped (optional)

sprig of flat leaf parsley, to garnish

1 Cook the potatoes in boiling, salted water for 15-20 minutes until tender.

2 Whisk together yogurt, spices and seasoning.

3 Drain the potatoes and immediately stir into the dressing. Leave to cool, then cover and refrigerate until 20 minutes before required.

4 Bring the salad back to room temperature. Just before serving, stir in the chillies, if using. Serve at room temperature, garnished with parsley.

133 CALORIES PER SERVING

SPICY SUMMER VEGETABLE SALAD

SERVES 4

115 g (4 oz) fromage frais

3 × 15 ml tbs low-fat French dressing

½ × 5 ml tsp garam masala

225 g (8 oz) new potatoes

175 g (6 oz) French beans, trimmed

1 large cauliflower, cut into florets

175 g (6 oz) mangetout, trimmed

1 large red pepper, seeded and quartered

chopped fresh parsley and coriander

lettuce leaves, to serve

1 For the dressing, blend the fromage frais, French dressing and garam masala together in a bowl. Leave to stand.

2 Steam the potatoes for about 25 minutes, the French beans for about 15 minutes, the cauliflower for about 10 minutes and the mangetout for about 5 minutes, until they are all just tender or *al dente*.

3 Grill the pepper, skin side up, under a hot grill until blackened. Cover with a damp tea-towel and leave until cool enough to handle. Peel, discard the skin and slice.

4 Halve the potatoes. Slice the cauliflower florets. Slice the mangetout into diagonal strips. Cut the French beans in half crosswise. Combine with the red pepper, parsley and coriander.

5 Mix the vegetables with the dressing. Pile on to a platter lined with the lettuce leaves.

148 CALORIES PER SERVING

Top: Cucumber and Watercress Salad
Middle: Spiced Potato Salad
Bottom: Spicy Summer Vegetable Salad

WINTER SALADS

....

*Crisp and crunchy salads, using raw or
lightly cooked ingredients like leeks,
cauliflower and fennel, make a pleasant
change from hot vegetable
accompaniments in the middle of winter.
Try serving the tasty winter salads in this
chapter with your favourite meat and fish
dishes, or as a light meal on their own.*

Top: Spiced Ratatouille Salad (page 72)
Bottom: Stir-Fry Leek Salad (page 78)

Spiced Ratatouille Salad

SERVES 10–12

450 g (1 lb) aubergines, roughly chopped

salt and pepper

450 g (1 lb) fresh tomatoes

3 × 15 ml tbs olive oil

225 g (8 oz) onion, skinned and roughly chopped

1 green pepper, halved, seeded and chopped

1 red pepper, halved, seeded and chopped

½ × 5 ml tsp chilli powder

2 garlic cloves, skinned and crushed

450 g (1 lb) courgettes, sliced

400 g can chopped tomatoes

1 × 5 ml tsp dried oregano

2 bay leaves

1 × 15 ml tbs vinegar

sprigs of fresh herbs, to garnish

1 Place the aubergines in a colander, sprinkle with salt and leave for 20-30 minutes. Rinse, drain and dry on absorbent kitchen paper.

2 Skin the tomatoes, quarter and seed, reserving the juices; roughly chop the flesh.

3 Heat the oil in a flameproof casserole. Add the onion, aubergines, peppers and chilli powder and stir-fry over a high heat for 2-3 minutes.

4 Mix in the fresh tomatoes and all the remaining ingredients. Bring to the boil, cover and simmer for 30-40 minutes until all the vegetables are soft and the liquid reduced. Adjust seasoning.

5 Cool; refrigerate well before serving, garnished with fresh herbs.

88-74 CALORIES PER SERVING

Pasta Salad with Avocado Dressing

SERVES 6

225 g (8 oz) pasta shapes

salt and pepper

115 g (4 oz) asparagus, trimmed, tips removed and stalks cut into 2.5 cm (1 in) pieces

2 courgettes, trimmed and sliced

1 large ripe avocado

200 g (7 oz) very low-fat fromage frais

1 × 15 ml tbs lemon juice

1 garlic clove, skinned and crushed

1 eating apple

2 × 15 ml tbs chopped fresh coriander

15 g (½ oz) shelled pistachios, chopped

1 Cook the pasta shapes in plenty of boiling salted water, according to the packet instructions.

2 Then 7 minutes before the end of the cooking time add the asparagus stalk pieces. Add the courgettes and asparagus tips 2-3 minutes before the end of the cooking time.

3 When the pasta is cooked, drain well, rinse under cold running water then drain well again. Place in a large bowl.

4 Cut the avocado in half, remove the stone then scoop out the flesh from one half and mash in a bowl. Add the fromage frais, lemon juice, garlic and salt and pepper and mix well together.

5 Chop the remaining avocado half into small pieces. Core and chop the apple. Pour the avocado dressing over the pasta and add the chopped avocado and apple. Toss together until mixed, then sprinkle with the coriander and pistachios. Serve at once.

235 CALORIES PER SERVING

Pasta Salad with Avocado Dressing

Deliciously Lean

Fresh Spinach
and
Baby Corn Salad

SERVES 8

335 g (12 oz) baby spinach
175 g (6 oz) fresh baby sweetcorn
50 ml (2 fl oz) olive oil
1 garlic clove, skinned and crushed
1 × 15 ml tbs white wine vinegar
2 × 5 ml tsp Dijon mustard
1 × 5 ml tsp caster sugar
salt and pepper
115 g (4 oz) alfalfa sprouts
1 head of chicory, trimmed and shredded

1 Wash the spinach well in several changes of cold water. Remove any coarse stalks. Drain well and pat dry on absorbent kitchen paper.

2 Halve the sweetcorn cobs lengthways. Cook in boiling water for about 3-5 minutes until just tender. Drain under cold running water.

3 Whisk together the olive oil, garlic, vinegar, mustard and sugar. Season with salt and pepper to taste.

4 Mix together the spinach, sweetcorn, alfalfa sprouts and chicory, toss in the dressing and serve immediately.

82 CALORIES PER SERVING

COOK'S TIP

If fresh baby sweetcorn are not available, use the pre-cooked canned variety.

Fresh Spinach and Baby Corn Salad

WILD RICE AND THYME SALAD

SERVES 8

150 g (5 oz) French beans, trimmed and halved

150 g (5 oz) broad beans, podded

salt and pepper

50 g (2 oz) wild rice

175 g (6 oz) long-grain brown rice

2 × 15 ml tbs grapeseed oil

50 g (2 oz) small button mushrooms, wiped

2 × 15 ml tbs chopped fresh thyme

1 × 15 ml tbs walnut oil

2 × 15 ml tbs white wine vinegar

1 × 15 ml tbs Dijon mustard

sprigs of fresh thyme, to garnish

1 Cook the French beans in a saucepan of boiling water for 10-12 minutes until just tender. Drain under cold running water and set aside to cool.

2 Cook the broad beans in a pan of boiling salted water for 5-7 minutes until just tender. Drain under cold running water, slipping off their outer skins if wished, and set aside to cool.

3 Place the wild rice in a large pan of boiling salted water. Boil for 10 minutes before adding the brown rice. Boil together for a further 25-30 minutes or until both are just tender. Drain the rice under cold running water.

4 Stir together the French beans, broad beans and rice in a large bowl.

5 Heat the grapeseed oil in a small frying pan and fry the mushrooms with the thyme for 2-3 minutes. Remove from the heat, stir in the walnut oil, vinegar, mustard and seasoning. Add to the rice mixture and stir well. Adjust the seasoning. Cool, cover and refrigerate until required. Serve garnished with sprigs of fresh thyme.

170 CALORIES PER SERVING

Wild Rice and Thyme Salad

CAULIFLOWER, BROCCOLI AND PEPPER SALAD

SERVES 6

225 g (8 oz) broccoli, trimmed and cut into florets

225 g (8 oz) cauliflower, cut into florets

1 small yellow pepper, seeded and thinly sliced

1 small red pepper, seeded and thinly sliced

1 garlic clove, skinned and crushed

4 × 15 ml tbs tahini (sesame seed paste)

4 × 15 ml tbs water

6 × 15 ml tbs lemon juice

salt and pepper

sesame seeds, to garnish

1 Blanch the broccoli and cauliflower in a saucepan of boiling water for 3 minutes, then drain and leave to cool. Place the broccoli, cauliflower and peppers in a salad bowl.

2 To make the dressing, whisk the garlic, tahini, water, lemon juice and seasoning together.

3 Pour the dressing over the salad and toss gently to coat. Cover and chill. Sprinkle with sesame seeds just before serving.

137 CALORIES PER SERVING

FENNEL AND CUCUMBER SALAD

SERVES 6

2 × 15 ml tbs caster sugar

50 ml (2 fl oz) lemon juice

50 ml (2 fl oz) olive oil

salt and pepper

3 large bulbs of fennel, total weight about 675 g (1½ lb)

3 × 15 ml tbs chopped fresh parsley

1 cucumber

1 Whisk together the sugar, lemon juice, olive oil and seasoning.

2 Trim the leafy ends from the fennel and finely chop them. Stir into the lemon and oil dressing mixture with the fresh parsley.

3 Thinly slice the fennel and cucumber. Toss in the herb dressing until the salad is thinly but evenly coated. Cover and refrigerate for at least 1 hour, preferably overnight.

115 CALORIES PER SERVING

VARIATION

Substitute three medium cucumbers for the fennel. It may sound a lot, but the thinly sliced cucumber softens down quite considerably in the dressing.

RICE AND KIDNEY BEAN SALAD

SERVES 4

225 g (8 oz) long-grain brown rice

salt and pepper

low-fat French dressing to moisten

220 g can red kidney beans, drained

a few salad onions, trimmed and chopped

½ cucumber, diced

2-3 celery sticks, trimmed and sliced

chopped fresh parsley, to garnish

1 Cook the rice in a saucepan of boiling salted water for 20 minutes until tender. Drain.

2 While the rice is still warm, add enough French dressing to moisten and stir in the kidney beans. Leave to cool.

3 Mix in the salad onions, cucumber, celery, parsley and seasoning.

270 CALORIES PER SERVING

Top: Fennel and Cucumber Salad
Middle: Cauliflower, Broccoli and Pepper Salad
Bottom: Rice and Kidney Bean Salad

WINTER SALAD

SERVES 4

1 lemon

2 × 15 ml tbs olive oil

150 ml (5 fl oz) low-fat natural yogurt

salt and pepper

2 eating apples, cored and roughly chopped

225 g (8 oz) red cabbage, thinly sliced

1 small onion, skinned and thinly sliced

4 celery sticks, trimmed and thinly sliced

115 g (4 oz) low-fat Cheddar-type cheese, cut into cubes

50 g (2 oz) unsalted peanuts in skins

celery leaves, to garnish (optional)

1 In a large bowl whisk together the grated rind of ½ lemon, 3 × 15 ml tbs lemon juice, the olive oil and yogurt. Season well.
2 Toss the chopped apples in the dressing.
3 Toss all the ingredients, except peanuts and celery leaves with the apples, mixing well. Sprinkle with peanuts and garnish with celery leaves, if liked.

285 CALORIES PER SERVING

STUFFED FENNEL SALAD

SERVES 4

4 bulbs of fennel

1 × 5 ml tsp olive oil

1 onion, skinned and chopped

1 garlic clove, skinned and chopped

227 g can chopped tomatoes

25 g (1 oz) stuffed green olives, chopped

salt and pepper

1 Snip off any green leafy tops from the fennel and reserve. Trim the hard cores off then split the bulbs in half lengthways.
2 Put the fennel bulbs in a pan of boiling water, return to the boil, then cook for 3 minutes. Drain.
3 Cut out the centre of each fennel bulb, then chop the scooped-out fennel.

4 Heat the oil in a saucepan, add the onion and cook for 10 minutes, until soft and golden. Add the chopped fennel and garlic and cook for a further 2-3 minutes. Add the tomatoes, olives, salt and pepper and simmer for 10 minutes.
5 Arrange the fennel halves in a shallow serving dish and fill with the tomato mixture. When cold, chill in the refrigerator for 2-3 hours. Serve garnished with the reserved fennel leaves.

60 CALORIES PER SERVING

STIR-FRIED LEEK SALAD

SERVES 4–6

900 g (2 lb) small leeks, trimmed

4 × 15 ml tbs olive oil

1 garlic clove, skinned and finely chopped

1 × 15 ml tbs wine vinegar

2 × 5 ml tsp wholegrain mustard

salt and pepper

1 hard-boiled egg, shelled

2 × 15 ml tbs snipped fresh chives

25 g (1 oz) walnut pieces

1 Finely slice the leeks into rounds then wash thoroughly. Drain well.
2 Heat 1 × 15 ml tbs oil in a large non-stick frying pan. Add the leeks and garlic and cook for 5 minutes until slightly softened but not browned, stirring frequently. Place in a shallow serving dish and leave to cool.
3 In a small bowl, put the remaining oil, the vinegar, mustard and salt and pepper and whisk together until well blended. Finely chop the egg and stir into the dressing with the chives.
4 Pour the dressing over the leeks and toss together. Chill in the refrigerator before serving. Serve sprinkled with the walnut pieces.

298-198 CALORIES PER SERVING

Top: Stuffed Fennel Salad
Bottom: Winter Salad

INDEX